Declarations of the Kingdom Driven Entrepreneur

Using your words to create an atmosphere of success for your business

Candace N. Ford

Foreword by
Shae Bynes and Antonina D. Geer
Co-Founders, Kingdom Driven Entrepreneur ™

Declarations of the Kingdom Driven Entrepreneur

ISBN 978-0989632249

Copyright 2013 by Kingdom Driven LLC
All rights reserved.

Published by Kingdom Driven Publishing
4846 N. University Drive #406
Lauderhill, FL 33351

Printed in the United States of America

All rights reserved. No portion of this book may be reproduced by any means - electronic, mechanical, photocopy, recording, scanning, or other - except for brief quotations in reviews or articles, without the prior written permission of the publisher. Your support of the authors' rights is appreciated.

Dedication

I would like to dedicate this book to Kingdom Driven Entrepreneurs who are walking in God's will to dominate the marketplace! I applaud you for taking the appropriate steps for God to use you in such a unique way.

Thank You!

Your purchase of this book is benefitting the Kingdom Driven Entrepreneur Harvest Fund. Thank you for your contribution!

The Harvest Fund provides cash awards to help Kingdom Driven Entrepreneurs worldwide with a variety of investments to help them start or grow their businesses.

Launched in November 2012, the Harvest Fund has already served as a blessing to many – both the contributors as well as the recipients. Kingdom Driven Entrepreneurs are radical givers and there is power in sowing seed into good ground!

For more details, visit
http://KingdomDrivenEntrepreneur.com/harvest

Thank you again for your support!

Contents

Foreword	1
Introduction	3
Mentors - Elijah's in Business	4
New in Business	6
A Profitable Business	8
Business Connections	11
Enlarge My Territory	13
Wisdom in Business	15
Business Strategies	17
Business Development & Growth	19
Leadership Skills	21
Business Sector & Industry Leadership	23
Branding	25
Marketing	27
Customer service	29
Social Media	31
Radical Giving	33
Debt Free Business	35
Time Management	37
Hiring, Delegation, People Management	40
Innovation	43
Conclusion	45
About the Author	46
Prayer Warriors for the Marketplace	48
About Kingdom Driven Entrepreneur	49
Books for Kingdom Driven Entrepreneurs	50

Foreword

As a Kingdom Driven Entrepreneur, you simply cannot do business as usual. To build a thriving business that serves your family, truly impacts lives, and advances the Kingdom of God in the marketplace you will need to operate in radical faith and radical obedience to the leading of the Holy Spirit.

James 2:14 makes it clear that true faith requires action. Seeking the Lord, obeying His instructions, and declaring your preferred future while keeping your eyes fixed upon Him are key actions to experience God's best for you in your life and business.

This book is full of powerful declarations to help you use your words (and the word of God) to create an atmosphere of success in your business.

Author Candace N. Ford is an unapologetically bold leader and visionary who is helping cultivate Kingdom leaders in the marketplace globally. She's no-nonsense, which is what we love about her. She compels you to action, and she does it all out of her love for God's people.

This is a devotional that you'll keep close by and reference often. The declarations and prayers are powerful and cover a variety of critical aspects of doing business...and doing it God's way.

When you place God in His proper position in your business – at the Head as the ultimate CEO – and you allow the Holy Spirit to lead you in your daily operations, you will enjoy one amazing adventure that will positively impact not only your family, but so many other lives as you fulfill your God-given assignment.

Expect the great. God is doing something unprecedented. Simply do your part (seek, trust, and obey). He has already done His.

>	Shae Bynes and Antonina Geer
>	Founders, Kingdom Driven Entrepreneur
>	KingdomDrivenEntrepreneur.com

Introduction

The word declare is defined as "to make known or state clearly, to announce officially; proclaim and to state emphatically". To make a declaration to others, states who you are, states what you will do and how you will get it done. The very act of declaration can be in writing but most declarations are spoken. Proverbs 18:21 states the tongue has the power of life and death and those who love it will eat its fruit.

As Kingdom Driven Entrepreneurs it is not only important to walk in integrity in what you do, but also in what you say. The words spoken over your business from your mouth will either cause success to your company or failure. That is why it is important to declare the word of God daily over your business endeavors.

As God's people we are made in His image and His likeness and just as God created the world with His words, we need to do the same. As entrepreneurs we should declare that we are the head and not the tail, above and not beneath, blessed in the city and blessed in the field. Moreover we should specifically declare that our businesses will advance the Kingdom of God and bring glory to God's name in the marketplace.

By speaking the declarations of this book over your business, I believe that God will answer your prayers and harken to His word, giving you the tools and resources to be a successful Kingdom Driven Entrepreneur.

Mentors – Elijah's in Business

II Kings 2:1-3 (NIV) When the Lord was about to take Elijah up to heaven in a whirlwind, Elijah and Elisha were on their way from Gilgal. 2 Elijah said to Elisha, "Stay here; the Lord has sent me to Bethel. "But Elisha said, "As surely as the Lord lives and as you live, I will not leave you." So they went down to Bethel. The company of the prophets at Bethel came out to Elisha and asked, "Do you know that the Lord is going to take your master from you today?" "Yes, I know," Elisha replied, "so be quiet."

In the Old Testament there was a Prophet by the name of Elijah who was very instrumental in training and preparing other Prophets in the way in which they should conduct themselves in releasing the word of the Lord to the nation of Israel. Elijah headed a Company of Prophets, mentoring them in the business of the Prophetic.

As Kingdom Driven Entrepreneurs we are also in need of mentors in the marketplace. These individuals will walk us through the process of ensuring that we are operating our business the Kingdom way and not in the way of the world. Those who are more experienced in entrepreneurship need to give back to others who are coming up in the ranks to become successful in their endeavors.

The world will know us not by our balance sheet or how many cars or homes we have; the world will know that we belong to God by the way we show love to one another. What greater way to show God's love than to help our fellow entrepreneurs become successful in what God has called them to do!

Declaration for Seasoned Entrepreneur

Father I declare that with what I have learned through others in the business arena you will provide opportunities for me to mentor others in doing business the Kingdom Way. Father I declare that I will not be stingy with my gifts nor my wisdom and I will pour back wisdom and knowledge into the next generation of entrepreneurs so that they might prevent making unnecessary mistakes. Father I thank You for the opportunities to mentor others in business and I praise You in advance that they will shine brighter and be successful in what You have given their hands to do.

Declaration for Entrepreneur Desiring A Mentor

Father I thank You now for my Elijah in Business. I thank You Father that you have given that individual the wisdom and insight I need to be successful in advancing the Kingdom of God in the marketplace. I declare right now that their business is flourishing and that they are available, ready and able to impart the anointing of entrepreneurship in my spirit so that I may one day be a mentor to others.

New In Business

2 Corinthians 5:17 Therefore, if anyone is in Christ, the new creation has come: The old has gone, the new is here!

Isaiah 43:19 (NIV) See, I am doing a new thing! Now it springs up; do you not perceive it? I am making a way in the wilderness and streams in the wasteland.

So many emotions, ideas and concerns arise when walking into something new. Transitioning from being an employee to a business owner can be exhilarating and at times quite scary. Thoughts run through your mind such as "Will I be able to sell enough products or services to live and provide for my family?" "Will my business ideas be welcomed in the market?" "Will I be a successful entrepreneur?" So many questions, but remember there is only one answer and that is God.

When God calls you to the pulpit of entrepreneurship and you answer, you must trust that the Lord will give you the tools and resources you need to be successful in that which He is calling you to do. God is a great provider and if He provided for you through your bi-weekly paycheck as an employee, why would He not be able to provide for you as a Kingdom Driven Entrepreneur? So go ahead, embrace the new, work hard at making your business successful and depend of God to supply all of your needs according to His riches in glory!

Declaration:

Father I thank You for this season of transition. I thank You for making all things new in my life and for allowing me to experience the new things that You want to do through me. I am honored to accept the call to the marketplace to represent Your Kingdom. Lord I ask that You give me the wisdom and insight needed to be successful in my calling. I thank You Father that everything I put my hands to is blessed and that through Your son Jesus I can do all things as He gives me strength. I declare today that I will advance Your Kingdom through my business endeavors and I will bring Your name glory in every activity of my business.

A Profitable Business

I Chronicles 21:22-24 (NIV) David said to him, "Let me have the site of your threshing floor so I can build an altar to the LORD, that the plague on the people may be stopped. Sell it to me at the full price." Araunah said to David, "Take it! Let my lord the king do whatever pleases him. Look, I will give the oxen for the burnt offerings, the threshing sledges for the wood, and the wheat for the grain offering. I will give all this." But King David replied to Araunah, "No, I insist on paying the full price. I will not take for the LORD what is yours, or sacrifice a burnt offering that costs me nothing."

God wants everything you put your hands to, to be profitable. Our God loves profit! When God made the earth He wanted mankind to dominate the resources that He'd placed in it and cause multiplication to it -- not just addition, but multiplication. He wanted Adam and Eve to take a seed and plant it so it could harvest as a tree -- not as one piece of fruit, but a tree of fruit.

Therefore in doing business as heirs to the throne of grace, we must remember that we are serving a God who wants our business to be profitable. But He never wants that profit to be your God. *Deuteronomy 8: 17-18 reads, And thou say in thine heart, My power and the might of mine hand hath gotten me this wealth. But thou shalt remember the*

Lord thy God: for it is he that giveth thee power to get wealth, that he may establish his covenant which he sware unto thy fathers, as it is this day. Moses warned the Children of Israel, when the wealth comes don't you forget who gave you the power to get it. This same caution is given to the Church by Jesus, when He told the disciples "you cannot serve two masters, because you will love one and hate (love the other one less), so you must only serve one."

We must remember that God is the source for our businesses and He supplies the resources we need to be successful in our business endeavors.
When you put God first, you will never have to worry about your business being in the red. When you put God first, you will never have to worry about missing a sale, and you will always be profitable.

Declaration:

Jesus I declare with my mouth that my Kingdom advancing enterprise is profitable and that the revenue made through my company greatly outweighs the cost that it took for the production of the products and the time spent in service to my clients. Father I declare that as my business operates in the black that I will not forget to give You praise for giving me the power to obtain the wealth. I will not serve the god of mammon; no Lord, You will be my only God! Father I partner with You now, knowing that my enterprises will be successful.

I declare that I believe every word that You have spoken in Your written word and released in the prophetic voice; that everything I put my hands to shall prosper and I will reap a harvest to be reseeded back into the Kingdom! There shall be no lack in my business because it is BACKED by Heaven's resources.

Business Connections

Amos 3:3 (KJV) Can two walk together, except they be agreed?

Matthew 18:19-20 (KJV) "Again, truly I tell you that if two of you on earth agree about anything they ask for, it will be done for them by my Father in heaven. For where two or three gather in my name, there am I with them."

How do I know who to connect with in business? Will they understand the uniqueness of my business? Will they want to steal my ideas? Will they want the same level of success that I desire?

A connection is something that joins; it's a relationship in which one is linked or bonded with someone else. When making business connections, you must ask God for discernment in order to recognize or perceive clearly who you should connect with as business partners or associations. These connections should offer wisdom and resources needed for you to be successful and you should be willing to do the same. These connections should increase you as you increase them.

As an entrepreneur you do not have time to be weighed down by doubt or fear, especially the doubt and fear of others. You must be led by God when connecting with others in the marketplace.

Declaration:

Father I declare that I am honored to be a Kingdom Driven Entrepreneur. I count it a privilege to serve the Kingdom of God through the marketplace. I declare that everything I do in business will please You, including the connections that I make with others. I speak right now that my clients, vendors, and business partners are connected with my enterprise to ensure that my business is profitable and that there is more seed to advance the Kingdom financially.

Father I dispel the enemy's plans as he would try to send wolves in sheep's clothing to try to cause confusion or dissension in my business connections and I declare that those who have been assigned to assist me and those You have assigned me to assist in business will be revealed in due season so that Your name will get all the glory and the praise.

Enlarge My Territory

Genesis 1:28 (KJV) And God blessed them, and God said unto them, Be fruitful, and multiply, and replenish the earth, and subdue it: and have dominion over the fish of the sea, and over the fowl of the air, and over every living thing that moveth upon the earth.

1 Chronicles 4:9-11 (NIV) Jabez was more honorable than his brothers. His mother had named him Jabez, saying, "I gave birth to him in pain." Jabez cried out to the God of Israel, "Oh, that you would bless me and enlarge my territory! Let your hand be with me, and keep me from harm so that I will be free from pain." And God granted his request.

As a Kingdom Ambassador, God has assigned you a tract of spiritual "land" and influence that must be dominated. As a Kingdom Driven Entrepreneur, this territory is defined by your selling activity in the marketplace. Since we serve a big God, we should never be afraid to ask our Father to expand our territory of influence. That is why God made man -- to dominate the entire earth and subdue its resources in order that the Kingdom of Heaven could be seen in all parts of the earth. Your marketplace anointing and the prayer of Jabez will allow God to make your name and His great in the earth!

Declaration:

Father I declare today an enlargement of my territory, the sphere of influence that You want me to dominate as it relates to my business. I believe Father that You have no respect of persons so as You enlarged the territory of Jabez, Lord I believe that You are more than able to do it for me.
I thank You Father for Your favor, mercy and grace and I praise You even the more for the strategies and plans that You download into my spirit man daily so that my business will operate in the success backed by Heaven. Lord I lay down all doubt and fear and trust that as I am faithful over the little You have given me thus far, that You will now make me ruler over MORE! In Jesus' name, Amen!

Wisdom in Business

Proverbs 4:6-8 (NIV) Do not forsake wisdom, and she will protect you; love her, and she will watch over you. The beginning of wisdom is this: Get wisdom. Though it cost all you have, get understanding. Cherish her, and she will exalt you; embrace her, and she will honor you.

I Kings 4:29-30 (NIV) God gave Solomon wisdom and very great insight, and a breadth of understanding as measureless as the sand on the seashore. Solomon's wisdom was greater than the wisdom of all the people of the East, and greater than all the wisdom of Egypt.

Wisdom is God and God is wisdom! That is why the Word of God says wisdom is the principal thing. Gaining wisdom in business is acknowledging that God is the most important component of your Kingdom enterprise. Wisdom is an asset that never depreciates and it always causes you as an entrepreneur to grow in your understanding of how to operate your business the way God wants you to.

When God asked Solomon what he needed to be a great King, Solomon simply asked for Wisdom. Although he did some really odd things in his personal life, God granted him the wisdom needed to properly operate as the King of Israel, and because of his unselfish request God made sure that his treasury never ran dry.

As a Kingdom Driven Entrepreneur you should be wise and ask for the wisdom you need to run your business efficiently, the wisdom you need to grow your business, the wisdom you need to provide proper product and services to your customers, as well as the wisdom needed to run your household and to find the necessary balance between family and work that is needed. Don't ask for wisdom only in one area, but in all areas because all of these areas will affect the growth or demise of your business.

Declaration:

Today I declare that I have the wisdom of God living and operating on the inside of me. Father I ask that through Your Spirit I will always know what to do when faced with challenges in my business or within my home.

I declare that I have the wisdom needed to grow my business, to make sound business decisions, to make covenant connections and to be a continual blessing to the Kingdom of God. I declare that wisdom is my portion and I receive it to be a prospering Kingdom Driven Entrepreneur.

Business Strategies

I Samuel 30: 7-8 (NIV) Then David said to Abiathar the priest, the son of Ahimelek, "Bring me the ephod." Abiathar brought it to him, and David inquired of the LORD, "Shall I pursue this raiding party? Will I overtake them?" "Pursue them," he answered. "You will certainly overtake them and succeed in the rescue."

Acts 13:22 (KJV) And when he had removed him, he raised up unto them David to be their king; to whom also he gave their testimony, and said, I have found David the son of Jesse, a man after mine own heart, which shall fulfil all my will.

The Word of God says that David was a man after God's on heart. In his young age he trusted God for provision and strategies to defeat the enemy. As he stood before Goliath he didn't destroy him with a sword but with a stone and a slingshot. As he grew older and became the King, David was faced with much opposition, externally and internally.

In the account in I Samuel 30, David returns from war to discover his wife, children, and the families of the other soldiers had been kidnapped by the enemy. In this extremely challenging situation David did not move in his flesh; he inquired of the Lord and asked what strategy to implement in order to be successful. David clearly asked the Lord "Should I go up, and if I go up will I recover what was stolen from me?" And the Lord answered him, yes go and recover ALL!

You cannot run a successful Kingdom enterprise without consulting God for strategies, because God is a planner. He is a designer and He is truly strategic in everything that He does. God making Adam was strategic, God sending Jesus was strategic and God making you an entrepreneur was strategic. So don't think for one second you can operate your business without consulting the Master Strategist. God will give you the necessary plans and strategies to be successful and for you to see that you need Him in everything you do concerning your business.

Declaration:

Father I declare today that as the Lord of my life I will come to You in prayer regarding the necessary strategies for my business to be successful and for the wisdom on how to implement those strategies.
I declare that as I ask You will answer, as I knock You will open and as I seek I will find. I declare that You God will reveal what is the proper way to operate my business in the marketplace. I thank You that You reveal these plans to me as I need them, never hiding the how, what, where, when and why of the Kingdom endeavor that You have given me.

I declare that I will be obedient in the execution of these heavenly strategies so that my business can bring You glory in the earth and in the marketplace.

Business Development and Growth

Genesis 1:1-3 (KJV) In the beginning God created the heaven and the earth. And the earth was without form, and void; and darkness was upon the face of the deep. And the Spirit of God moved upon the face of the waters. And God said, Let there be light: and there was light.

John 1:1-3 (KJV) In the beginning was the Word, and the Word was with God, and the Word was God. The same was in the beginning with God. All things were made by him; and without him was not anything made that was made.

Generally speaking, business development is the creation of long-term value to enable business growth – leveraging opportunities and partnerships to drive greater revenue. Business development is God's expertise! He used this tool in Genesis 1 when He created the earth, the birds and the animals, when He put the trees and rivers in the right place and when He created human beings. He did this to develop and expand the business of Heaven here on earth.

Constant development and growth in your business is what God desires for you. He never wants His family business to go backwards, but it should always be increasing, adding on others and ADVANCING! So don't hesitate to take steps to develop your business, whether it be launching new products or offering new services. Allow God to anoint you with the ability to continue to supply the demand of the industry in which you service.

Declarations:

Father I declare today that I am made in the image and likeness of You; that I have Your creative power living on the inside of me to speak into existence the things that I need to be a successful entrepreneur. I declare that my tongue will speak life on the development of my product and service offerings, that my business will be first in innovative ideas, and that my business will advance the Kingdom of God through these undertakings.

Father I thank You for the ability to call things as though they will be and not what they are. I declare that as I am developed in Your word and the right way of doing business, my business will be established and have influence in the earth.

Leadership Skills

Matthew 4:18-20 And Jesus, walking by the sea of Galilee, saw two brethren, Simon called Peter, and Andrew his brother, casting a net into the sea: for they were fishers. And he saith unto them, Follow me, and I will make you fishers of men. And they straightway left their nets, and followed him.

Matthew 10:37-39 "Anyone who loves their father or mother more than me is not worthy of me; anyone who loves their son or daughter more than me is not worthy of me. Whoever does not take up their cross and follow me is not worthy of me. Whoever finds their life will lose it, and whoever loses their life for my sake will find it.

The anointing of leadership was embodied in the life of Jesus Christ. He had followers who followed Him not because they truly understood who He was, but because they saw for themselves that He had the ability to lead. He was gifted not just with charisma but with true Godly character. Jesus was the greatest leader because He was the greatest follower. He did nothing on the earth unless directed by His heavenly Father.

The ability to lead is born out of the ability to follow. Remember when you were an employee? Were you always late, did you fail to complete projects, disrespect your manager, and cause dissension with your co-workers? Well if the answer is yes, before you go into business as the owner you need to repent for your actions of being a horrible follower because you will definitely reap that harvest in your leadership. A leader is mature. A leader admits his or her mistakes. Leaders make sure their followers are developed and have what they need to be successful. Mirror the walk of Christ in order to develop your leadership skills. He is truly a great example.

Declaration:

Father I want to be more like Your Son. I declare that in the daily activities of my business, I will lead my enterprise and my employees in the Character of Christ, concerning myself more with the development of those under me than any of my own professional needs.

Father, I declare that I walk in maturity, in love, in forgiveness and patience in dealing with those who have been assigned to follow me. I thank You Father for molding and making me into a leader for providing the resources and tools that I need to put into place to ensure the growth of others. In Jesus' name, Amen!

Business Sector and Industry Leadership

Matthew 23: 1-4 (NIV) Then Jesus said to the crowds and to his disciples: "The teachers of the law and the Pharisees sit in Moses' seat. So you must be careful to do everything they tell you. But do not do what they do, for they do not practice what they preach. They tie up heavy, cumbersome loads and put them on other people's shoulders, but they themselves are not willing to lift a finger to move them.

    For a Kingdom Driven Entrepreneur, identifying your business sector and industry enables you to conduct effective research for target marketing, potential investment dollars and proper business strategies when moving into new markets. How can you be unique within your industry if you are unaware of the current trends of that industry?

    Jesus knew the industry of religion very well. He taught His disciples what not to partake in so they would never be affiliated with the teachings of the hypocrites. This is why Jesus stood out when He walked the earth; He'd studied the bankrupt industry of the religious system and delivered the products of Heaven – love, peace, healing, and grace which allowed many customers (followers) to come back for repeat business! Study your trade, study your business model and most importantly study your industry so that you can be the preferred supplier to the demand!

Declaration

Father I declare that my business is favored in the _____ industry.

As a Kingdom Driven Entrepreneur I believe You at Your word, Father, as it says I am blessed coming in and blessed going out and that I am the head and not the tail. I proclaim that my company, by the leading of the Holy Spirit, will create fresh and new ideas for the industry and that my company will be constantly innovative in bringing life-changing products and services to market.

Father I speak to the economy of this industry and I tell it to produce and be fruitful in the name of Jesus.

Branding

Genesis 1:26-27 (NIV) Then God said, "Let us make mankind in our image, in our likeness, so that they may rule over the fish in the sea and the birds in the sky, over the livestock and all the wild animals, and over all the creatures that move along the ground." So God created mankind in his own image, in the image of God he created them; male and female he created them.

Proverbs 3:3-4 (MSG) Don't lose your grip on Love and Loyalty. Tie them around your neck; carve their initials on your heart. Earn a reputation for living well in God's eyes and the eyes of the people.

A brand is the idea or image of a specific product or service that consumers connect with, by identifying the name, logo, slogan, or design of the company who owns the idea or image. The act of branding is when that idea or image is marketed so that it is recognizable by more and more people, and identified with a certain service or product.

Kingdom Driven Entrepreneurs are the products of the Jesus Christ brand! Everything that we do and how we do it in business derives from the attitude of "What would Jesus do?" We do not operate like the businesses of the world, gauging prices, cheating clients or suppliers. We operate from the vine as we are the branches producing the fruit of the

Spirit; love, joy, peace, forbearance, kindness, goodness, faithfulness, gentleness and self-control. The fruit has to be operating in our businesses because it is how we represent and prevent defaming the reputation of the brand of Jesus Christ.

Declaration:

Father I declare this day that as I develop my brand I will be led by the Holy Spirit. Holy Spirit give me the wisdom, revelation and insight as well as a branding firm that operates in the spirit of excellence. Father I declare that my brand and my company are favored in the marketplace. I worship You for allowing my brand to represent the Kingdom of God in the marketplace. I praise You Father for giving me the proper name for my company, for giving me the colors of my logo ,and the layout of my website. I thank You Lord for showing me the schematics of how my brand should be used in social media and at networking events.

I declare my brand shall bring Your name glory, in the name of Jesus, Amen!

Marketing

2 Corinthians 10:3-6 (MSG) The world is unprincipled. It's dog-eat-dog out there! The world doesn't fight fair. But we don't live or fight our battles that way—never have and never will. The tools of our trade aren't for marketing or manipulation, but they are for demolishing that entire massively corrupt culture. We use our powerful God-tools for smashing warped philosophies, tearing down barriers erected against the truth of God, fitting every loose thought and emotion and impulse into the structure of life shaped by Christ. Our tools are ready at hand for clearing the ground of every obstruction and building lives of obedience into maturity.

Marketing your business God's way is vitally important. You must seek His wisdom in identifying your product or service so that you know that what you are selling is what God has ordained for your business. Seek God in determining the price that will be fair to your customers and generate a profit for you. Ask God to show you the proper way to get the product and service to market so you may properly supply the demands of your target audience. Last but not least, seek the Lord for promotional strategies, what services and media outlets should be used to bring awareness to your business. Your greatest asset in your company is God -- go to Him for the market strategies you need to create a marketing plan that will generate great profits in your company.

Declaration:

Father I declare that I receive wisdom from the Holy Spirit on how to effectively market the products and services that You have put into my hand to be a blessing to the Kingdom of God through the marketplace. I trust Father that all that I need including marketing dollars, resources and favor will be provided by You.

Father I proclaim that each dollar spent in the marketing of my company will yield me seven clients. I declare with my mouth that my company's product, price, place of distribution channel and promotional strategies are all implemented in the spirit of excellence and integrity. In addition, as I market my company's offerings that Your name will be glorified. Father God I proclaim growth and the success of my business in the marketplace. In Jesus' Name, Amen!

Customer Service

Galatians 5:13-14(NIV) You, my brothers and sisters, were called to be free. But do not use your freedom to indulge the flesh; rather, serve one another humbly in love. For the entire law is fulfilled in keeping this one command: "Love your neighbor as yourself."

As a Kingdom Driven Entrepreneur your company should never deliver sub-par products or shoddy services. A business is nothing without its customers and can truly thrive only when its clients are satisfied with the products or services delivered. You are not in business to simply please the client, but you are in business so that God would be pleased with your life. Although the client may never see what you do behind the scenes, God always does. So allow God to be pleased with you from the beginning of the sale to the end. Let Him be pleased to call you His child as you operate in the spirit of excellence and integrity when doing the business of your business.

Declaration:

Father I thank You for my past, current and future clients. I thank You Lord that You have allowed my services and products to be placed in their hands to change their lives, families and businesses for the better. I now declare Lord that You give me wisdom and discernment on how to better communicate to my clients and to understand their problems so that my business can be their solution.

I declare that if there are any circumstances that are not profitable for either the company or the clients, that we can come to a peaceful conclusion of the matter, so that Your name will never be put to shame through the actions of my business. Father I humble myself to You as I deal with my customers. Give me strategies, give me new ideas, give me the patience and love necessary to do business WELL before Your eyes. In Jesus' Name. Amen!

Social Media

John 4:28-30 Then, leaving her water jar, the woman went back to the town and said to the people, "Come, see a man who told me everything I ever did. Could this be the Messiah?" They came out of the town and made their way toward him.

The first status posted through "social media" in the history of Jesus' ministry was done by the Woman at the Well! His conversation with her about her life and what she needed to change and most importantly who He was, caused her to go and tell everyone of a man who knew everything about her. Even when Jesus told her not to, because of the impact He had on her in that short amount of time, she had to make the announcement to the town. Our businesses should have this same impact on our clients, customers and suppliers -- that they will want to tell their community through Twitter, Facebook, LinkedIn, Instagram, Pinterest, and other social media platforms about the great experience they had with us in their business transaction.

Don't miss opportunities through social media to show Jesus in the marketplace. Don't be ashamed of being a Kingdom Driven Entrepreneur, and don't be ashamed to tell people that you are a business owner who is a Christian. God wants to show you off, and so you show Him off, in and throughout your media to society, current and potential clients.

Declaration:

Father I declare that the time and effort invested in building my company's social media platforms will cause awareness to those who You have assigned to my endeavors. I declare that the social media interactions that I have with current and future clients will yield great income for my business.

As You expand my territory through the various social media outlets I declare that my statuses, tweets, blogs, pictures and posts will cause others to see Your glory and the favor that rests on my business. I thank You Father for allowing me to be in business in the age of social media and interactive technology and I declare I will use these resources to grow my business.

Radical Giving

Genesis 8:22 (AMP) While the earth remains, seedtime and harvest, cold and heat, summer and winter, and day and night shall not cease.

II Corinthians 9:5-7 (NIV) So I thought it necessary to urge the brothers to visit you in advance and finish the arrangements for the generous gift you had promised. Then it will be ready as a generous gift, not as one grudgingly given. Remember this: Whoever sows sparingly will also reap sparingly, and whoever sows generously will also reap generously. Each of you should give what you have decided in your heart to give, not reluctantly or under compulsion, for God loves a cheerful giver.

Galatians 6:7-8 (NIV) Do not be deceived: God cannot be mocked. A man reaps what he sows. 8 Whoever sows to please their flesh, from the flesh will reap destruction; whoever sows to please the Spirit, from the Spirit will reap eternal life.

Sowing and reaping was a Law decreed by God in Genesis 8:22. When a Law is adopted, that Law cannot be overturned unless there is a higher authority put in position to change the Law. Since there will never be one greater than God, we must understand that this Law will work when put into action.

Kingdom Driven Entrepreneurs must understand that its imperative for your business to have a giving plan. You cannot say you represent God who is a giver and be stingy with your gifts. Money is seed, time is seed, wisdom is seed, love is seed, listening is seed -- these are the things that need to be planted in the lives and business of other Kingdom Driven Entrepreneurs and those who are on the ministry mission field for God.

Don't hold your seed back -- plant it into the Kingdom because the Law has been set!

Declaration:

Father in the name of Jesus I declare that I am a Kingdom Driven Entrepreneur who is a radical giver! I thank You that You give seed to the sower and as You give the seed Father I will be obedient to sow into whatever ground You direct me to sow into.

Father I declare that my sowing will cause others to be able to do what You have called them to do for the Kingdom and that as we all reap harvest, we can help build schools, orphanages, and homes in the name of our Lord.

Father I declare that the profits of my business will be used to further advance the Kingdom of God. I declare that I will not be stingy or selfish with my earnings and I declare that as You give me more, I will give more. I thank You for being the Lord of the Harvest and the Lord over the finances of my business. In Jesus' name Amen!

Debt Free Business

Romans 13:7-8 Give to everyone what you owe them: If you owe taxes, pay taxes; if revenue, then revenue; if respect, then respect; if honor, then honor. Let no debt remain outstanding, except the continuing debt to love one another, for whoever loves others has fulfilled the law.

In the society in which we live, it is extremely difficult to NOT be in debt. We as the citizens of the Kingdom of God WORK on earth, but we LIVE in Heaven. It is now time as Kingdom Driven Entrepreneurs that we begin to operate our business from the seated position that we have next to Christ in Heaven. We have to use the anointing of entrepreneurship to change the way business is conducted here on earth. We must be the head and not the tail and we need to be in the position to be the lender and not the borrower.

You do not have to go into debt to be in business. If God gave you the vision, He also supplies the provision. Follow the leading of the Holy Spirit in any instance when you are faced with the decision to obtain business capital or loans for large projects or business expansion. He is Your Provider with infinite resources available and He will direct you on how best to proceed.

Declaration:

Father I thank You for the ability and resources to operate my business debt free. I declare that as a child of God I am the head and not the tail, above and not beneath. I am the lender and not the borrower. I declare that the needs of my company are met whether it is for equipment, supplies, office rent or utilities. I declare that my home is debt free allowing me to invest into my business and the Kingdom of God so that it may be advanced.

Father allow me to circumcise my flesh regarding my spending habits and to strategize and plan out the cash of my business in order to make purchases using cash. Father I thank You for relieving my debt both spiritually and naturally In Jesus' name, AMEN!

Time Management

Romans 13:11-14 (MSG) But make sure that you don't get so absorbed and exhausted in taking care of all your day-by-day obligations that you lose track of the time and doze off, oblivious to God. The night is about over, dawn is about to break. Be up and awake to what God is doing! God is putting the finishing touches on the salvation work he began when we first believed. We can't afford to waste a minute, must not squander these precious daylight hours in frivolity and indulgence, in sleeping around and dissipation, in bickering and grabbing everything in sight. Get out of bed and get dressed! Don't loiter and linger, waiting until the very last minute. Dress yourselves in Christ, and be up and about!

Time is a precious commodity when you own and operate a business. The world emphatically declares that *"time is money!"* Time is an asset that, if wasted, you will surely never gain it back. We as Kingdom Driven Entrepreneurs have to be mindful of the time we spend building our businesses, as well as being mindful of the time we spend with God. Remember our natural time management is a result of how much time we spend developing ourselves.

For instance, when God says that it's time to launch a new product, are you slow to move or are you ready to take hold of the time? What about this...when God tells you it's NOT time to launch or start something how obedient are you so that you won't move outside of God's timing for your business? We must schedule our time wisely and before we fill up our appointment book with things to do for God, let us fill it up with spending time with God.

When I first started my business I would spend hours in researching software, reading articles, doing client work at the wee hours of the night because I believed the more time I spent in my business the more productive it would be. WRONG! I was tired, irritable, and could not maintain focus. Why? Because I was spending more time in the business than spending time with the God of my business.

I took the stance to make adjustments, I set reasonable work days and hours, and I stopped responding to emails at 1 a.m. I began to pray over my business and allow the Holy Spirit to give me strategies on how to operate my business, and then I began to feel productive. Yes time is valuable, but spending time with God regarding your business is priceless!!

Declaration:

Father today I declare that I will live with Matthew 6:33 as the foundation for my business and my life. Yes I will put You first, I will prioritize our time spent together so that I may know and understand how to efficiently operate in business. Father I thank You for the business endeavors that You have placed in my hand but I will not allow it to be more important than my relationship with You. I am honored that You have chosen me for the marketplace. As I lean more on the Holy Spirit for wisdom and guidance I know that the time spent in my business will be productive, allowing me to sow into the Kingdom of God.

Father I declare that I will know the seasons and the times in which You want me to launch or develop different products and services that need to be sold in the marketplace.

Father I declare that I know the seasons when to discontinue any product or service offerings in my business. I declare that I know the seasons and times of what You want to do in my business and I will use that time wisely. In Jesus' name, AMEN!

Hiring, Delegation, and People Management

Exodus 28:3 Tell all the skilled workers to whom I have given wisdom in such matters that they are to make garments for Aaron, for his consecration, so he may serve me as priest.

I Chronicles 22:14-16(NIV) "I have taken great pains to provide for the temple of the Lord a hundred thousand talents of gold, a million talents[c] of silver, quantities of bronze and iron too great to be weighed, and wood and stone. And you may add to them. You have many workers: stonecutters, masons and carpenters, as well as those skilled in every kind of work in gold and silver, bronze and iron—craftsmen beyond number. Now begin the work, and the Lord be with you." Then David ordered all the leaders of Israel to help his son Solomon.

    King David was a man after God's own heart. He loved the Lord and the Lord loved him. David desired to show his love to God by building His presence, a place to dwell, a place where His people could come and worship Him. But the Lord told David, because he was a Man of War and his hands were soaked in blood He would give favor to David's son Solomon to build the temple. And so Solomon was given the charge of building the temple of the Lord. Solomon was not equipped to do the project alone;

he had the grace to lead the building of the temple but not the learned knowledge to complete it in excellence. So what did He do? He hired people to assist, and not just people he knew or those who liked him, but people who were skilled in the building of buildings! He hired skilled masons because he loved God and wanted God to have the best.

You too have a place to build for God and it's called your BUSINESS and you know what? You cannot do it by yourself! There will come a time, as God blesses and expands your endeavors that you will need to hire, delegate and manage the skilled workers God has assigned to you. These workers will help you to get the job done in the spirit of excellence. A true entrepreneur understands that they cannot be successful in their business if they don't properly delegate to others. You will become burned out and frustrated because you are running the front, middle and back office. You will then become weary in doing well and want to give up and that is what happens to people who try to do it all by themselves. Begin to seek God for areas in your business that can be delegated and believe Him for the resources to fill that need.

Declaration:

Father I declare that I will be a good steward over the business that You have given me to advance Your Kingdom in the marketplace. I declare that I will be able to discern and properly delegate the work of the business to those skilled workers You have assigned to me. I bless my current and future employees and contract workers. I declare right now that their gifts will make room for them in my business.

I declare that they are sober minded, knowledgeable, hardworking and ready to assist with Your vision for the business. Father I declare that I am a wise leader, that I am able to assist the skilled workers when needed, and as a team we will give Your name glory in everything that the business produces. In Jesus' name, Amen!

Innovation

Proverbs 8:12 (KJV) I wisdom dwell with prudence, and find out knowledge of witty inventions.

I Corinthians 2: 15-16 15 The person with the Spirit makes judgments about all things, but such a person is not subject to merely human judgments, for, "Who has known the mind of the Lord so as to instruct him?" But we have the mind of Christ.

Matthew 10:16 (KJV) Behold, I send you forth as sheep in the midst of wolves: be ye therefore wise as serpents, and harmless as doves.

    Entrepreneurs for God's Kingdom are in this world but not of this world. This means although you operate in the same economy or industries in the earth, you are not to conduct your business like the world does. Why? Because you belong to God and you have the mind of Christ! Belonging to Christ does not make you weak, but rather it gives you the power, authority and the ability to tap into Kingdom resources that no sinner could have access to. Belonging to God and having the mind of Christ allows you to dream big and see the solution even before the problem arises.

    The mind of Christ allows you to perceive the future and allows your faith to soar into great possibilities and resources for your business.

So don't be afraid to tap into the spirit realm for the inventions and ideas that you need to be successful in the earth. You are God's child, you have the Holy Spirit living on the inside of you therefore you should have a clear picture of how God wants you to dominate the marketplace and should NOT be afraid to implement and launch whatever invention and idea that God has given you.

Declaration:

Father I declare right now that I have the mind of Christ and that I renew my mind daily to Your word, the written and the prophetic word, spoken over the success of my business. I thank You Father that every idea and invention that You have predestined for my life will be manifested in due season. I yield myself to You as You allow me to create and develop those things in the earth that will allow me to dominate the marketplace for the Kingdom of God.

I declare that nothing is missing, nothing is broken as I develop the products and services in which You have assigned to my hands. I declare that I am wise as a serpent and harmless as a dove. I declare I am the head and not the tail and I am favored in everything I do. Father I declare that as I am made in the image and likeness of You that I will create, I will develop, I will be the first to market and I will generate revenue to advance Your Kingdom in the Marketplace. In Jesus' name, Amen!

Conclusion

If you're not ready to fully trust God, you're not ready to be a Kingdom Driven Entrepreneur. The anointing of entrepreneurship requires you to believe and declare God's word and that takes a bold, radical faith! You can't be a punk, whiner, or complainer and be successful in what the Lord has called you to do as a Kingdom Driven Entrepreneur.

You must stand up strong knowing how to be content in God and the heavenly purpose for your business, whether you are abound or abased, full or hungry, in need or full of supply. It's an honor to advance the Kingdom of God through entrepreneurship so if this is your calling, you walk as bold as a lion, be wise as a serpent, yet harmless as a dove and go out and dominate your assigned territory of the marketplace!

Are you ready?

About The Author

Candace N. Ford is an entrepreneur, author, speaker, an ordained minister and spiritual strategist, who believes in producing multiple streams of income. Her and her husband, Apostle C. Kevin Ford are the governing apostle of Abiding Presence International Alliance, spiritually covering churches and para-church ministries across the nation. She is the CEO of Love Clones Publishing a full service publishing firm for aspiring and current authors, and the Dean of the Spiritual Development Institute, a place of training and discipling for Kingdom citizens.

Finally, Candace is a proud member of the Covenant Board of Kingdom Driven Entrepreneurs, an organization with a mission to activate a community of entrepreneurs that will demonstrate the power, presence, passion, and purity of God in the marketplace.

Graduating from DePaul University with a Bachelors of Science degree in Accountancy, she began work at PricewaterhouseCoopers, LLP as a financial auditor. Her accounting career continued with positions at various companies such as Sara Lee Corporation, Solomon Edwards Consulting and United Airlines. While working in the accounting field, she believed there was more for her to do to assist others, not financially, but spiritually. She began her first ministry to women in 2005.

Through CNF Ministries, Candace is dedicated to helping men and women acknowledge and develop their gifts and talents in the earth. Through teachings, workshops and one-on-one mentoring, she endeavors to cultivate kingdom leaders as they recognize their uniqueness in the marketplace or ministry while motivating them to maximize their leadership potential.

Candace and her husband live in Dallas, TX, with their son Nicholas and daughters, Brianna, Madison and Charis.

Visit Candace on the web at www.cnfministries.com

About Kingdom Driven Entrepreneur

Kingdom Driven Entrepreneur (KDE) has a mission to activate a community of entrepreneurs that will demonstrate the power, presence, passion, and purity of God in the marketplace.

It's more than a community – it's a movement! We are activating firestarters in the marketplace. Our role is to activate marketplace leaders and facilitate divine connections and collaboration through our online community (KingdomDrivenEntrepreneur.com) as well as offline through our live events and KDE Small Groups across the world. We equip entrepreneurs to do business God's way through training, the Kingdom Driven Entrepreneur Podcast, as well as our library of KDE books.

This isn't business as usual.

We invite you to join our community and get plugged in today at KingdomDrivenEntrepreneur.com!

Other Books for Kingdom Driven Entrepreneurs

The Kingdom Driven Entrepreneur: Doing Business God's Way (ISBN: 978-0615736129)

The Kingdom Driven Entrepreneur's Guide To Goal Setting (ISBN: 978-0615771892)

The Kingdom Driven Entrepreneur's Guide To Fearless Business Finance (ISBN: 978-0989632201)

The Kingdom Driven Entrepreneur's Guide To Holistic Health (ISBN: 978-0989632218)

Encountering God: A Devotional for the Kingdom Driven Entrepreneur (ISBN: 978-0989632225)

The Kingdom Driven Entrepreneur's Guide To Extraordinary Leadership (ISBN: 978-0989632232)

The Firestarter Effect: Making Jesus Christ Known in the Marketplace (ISBN: 978-0989632256)

The Firestarter Effect: Activating the Power of Covenant (ISBN: 978-0989632270)

Made in the USA
Middletown, DE
03 January 2020